T0055816

Concerto in D Minor for Piano and Band

Arranged for Two Pianos

By John Thompson

ISBN 978-1-4803-4464-8

WILLIS MUSIC

EXCLUSIVELY DISTRIBUTED BY

HAL•LEONARD® CORPORATION

7777 W. BLUEMOUND RD. P.O. BOX 13819 MILWAUKEE, WI 53213

Visit Hal Leonard Online at
www.halleonard.com

FOREWORD

This Concerto is designed for pupils of average High School age and is intended to serve as preparation for the study of the easier Concertos of the Masters.

It is scored for Piano and Band but can also be played on two pianos as this edition contains an arrangement of the band accompaniment for a second piano.

The first movement is written in sonata form and is built, for the most part, on passages familiar to pianists in this grade. The last two movements are based on the Pentatonic (five note) scale, sometimes known as the Scotch Scale. This, together with the Bag-Pipe effects in the accompaniment give a decidedly Scotch "flavor" to the work.

The experience gained in studying this Concerto should have a salutary effect and enable the pupil to approach the Master Concertos with more confidence and understanding. It has the happy faculty of sounding much more difficult than it really is and, properly played, can result in a very brilliant performance.

The Band accompaniment for this Concerto has been scored by the son of the composer, John Thompson, Jr., and is of Junior High, and High School level in difficulty.

A complete set of Band parts, as well as the Conductor's score is available from the Willis Music Company.

Concerto
in D minor

John Thompson

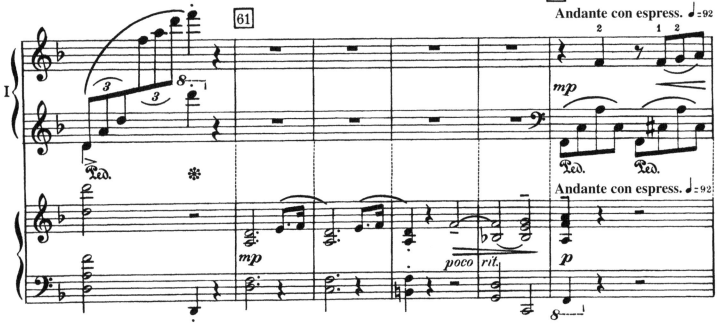

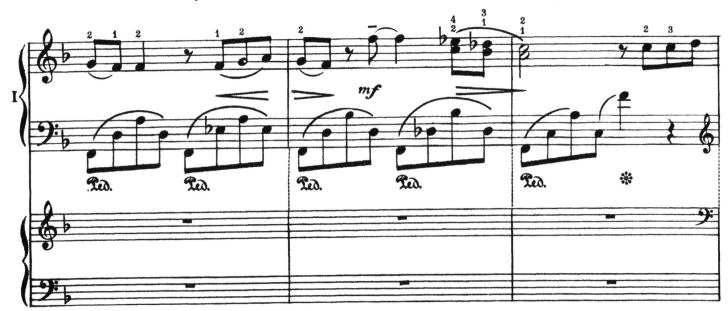

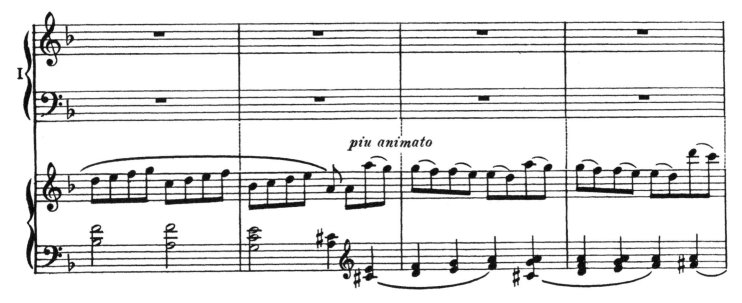

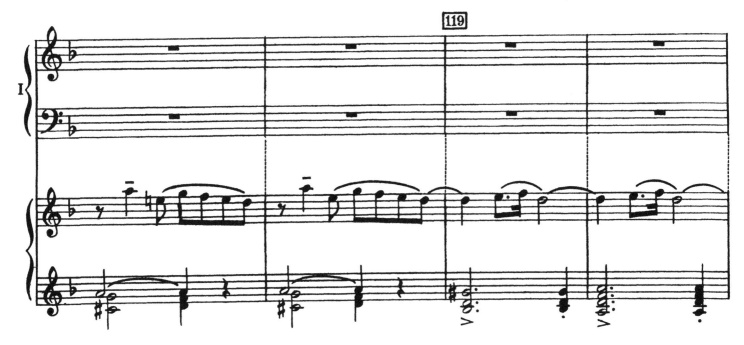

127 **Andante**

II

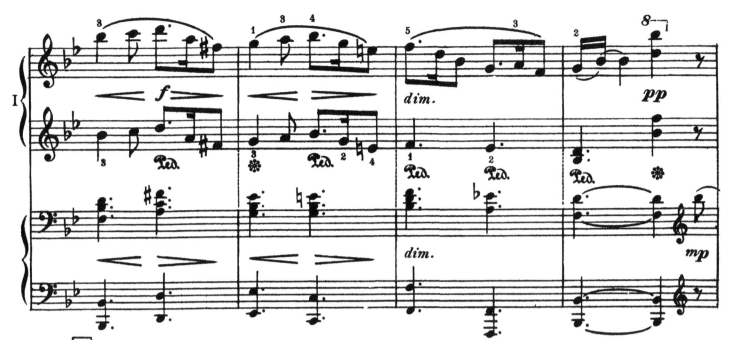

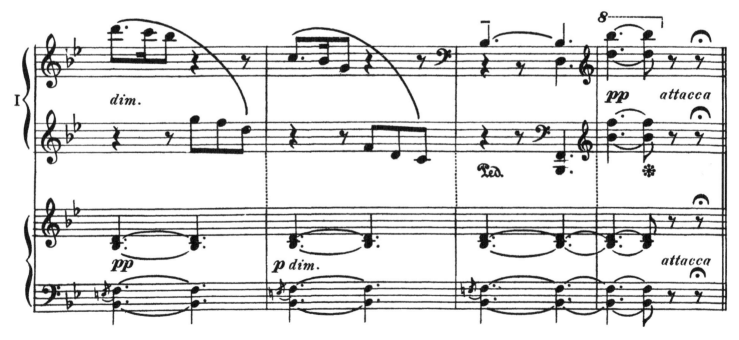

III

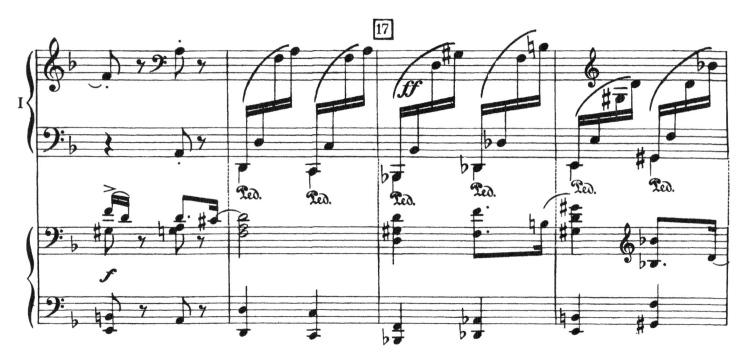

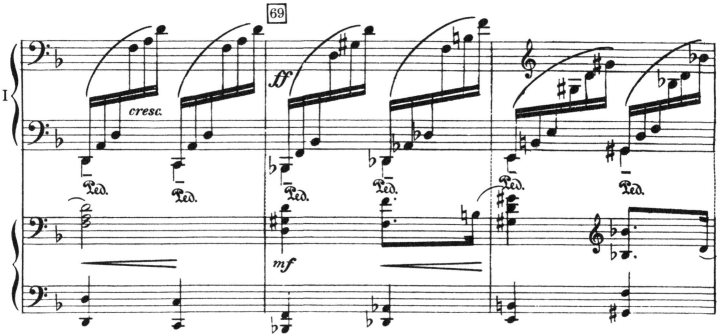